# SEVEN ONE-ACT PLAYS

BY
**WENDY WASSERSTEIN**

BETTE AND ME, WAITING FOR PHILIP GLASS,
TENDER OFFER, WORKOUT, MEDEA,
BOY MEETS GIRL AND THE MAN IN A CASE

★

★

DRAMATISTS
PLAY SERVICE
INC.

# TABLE OF CONTENTS

# DATE DUE

| | |
|---|---|
| JUL 2 1 2008 | |
| AUG 1 3 2009 | |
| SEP 1 7 2009 | |
| | |
| | |
| | |
| | |
| | |
| | |
| | |
| | |
| | |
| | |
| | |
| | |

# BETTE AND ME

## A MUSICAL FANTASY IN SEVEN SCENES

# BETTE AND ME

## A MUSICAL FANTASY IN SEVEN SCENES

## SCENE ONE

WENDY.   I am forty-five minutes late to meet Bette Midler. We
are meeting in her loft in Manhattan's Tr-Be-Ca. It happens to be
Gay Pride Day and the streets of Greenwich Village have been
quartered off by the NYPD for the parade. I am vaguely hysterical
and keep telling myself that if anyone will understand it will be
Bette who has been for decades a supporter and icon of the gay
community. I'm also having another little problem. I can't seem
to find her house. The building is way unassuming and not far
from the Holland Tunnel entrance. My taxi is trapped between
gay pride and Menlo Park Jersey commuters. When I finally arrive
The Divine Miss M. greets me at her self-service elevator. She is
wearing a silver lamé bikini and emerges on the half shell.

BETTE.   You're late.

WENDY.   You're wearing lamé.

BETTE.   I can't find my chandelier.

WENDY.   Have you lost it?

BETTE.   It makes such a nice hat.

WENDY.   But it's Sunday.

BETTE.   So.

WENDY.   I was just thinking you'd be slightly more informal.

BETTE.   I was thinking you'd be more on time.

WENDY.   I got stuck behind a parade.

BETTE.   Which one?

WENDY.   Gay Pride.

BETTE.   Then it's all right. Why are you staring at me?

WENDY.   You are everything I thought you would be. You are
everything everyone thinks you'd be.

BETTE.  Yes. I don't like to surprise anyone. I live strictly according to my stereotype. Do you like my song "Friends"?

WENDY.  It's wonderful!

BETTE.  Good. We'll sing it in the elevator.

WENDY.  Bette closes the elevator door. She hands me the sheet music of "Friends" as the elevator "Musak" begins playing the familiar tune. We sing together, "You've Got to Have Friends."*


## SCENE TWO


*Bette Midler's living room which has 50 purple lanterns on the ceiling and a view of the Hudson River.*


BETTE.  I wouldn't live anywhere but downtown. Would you like some Pellegrino water?

WENDY.  Sure.

BETTE.  Where do you live?

WENDY.  Uptown. But I think I should move back downtown.

BETTE.  Why don't you do what you want?

WENDY.  Because I don't have the confidence you have. Because I would never have the guts to cover my ceiling with purple lanterns. Because you have created a lovable larger-than-life personality and I am devoted to making mine smaller and smaller.

BETTE.  What are you talking about?

WENDY.  Everything we were told we shouldn't do as girls you were brave enough to do.

BETTE.  Are you sure you have the right apartment?

WENDY.  You're balsy, sassy, warm, sexy and let's face it you don't have the arms of Gwyneth Paltrow or Michelle Pfeiffer.

BETTE.  This is the strangest interview I've ever had.

* See Special Note on Songs and Recordings on copyright page.

WENDY.   I am obsessed with your confidence!

BETTE.   Do you take Prozac? Maybe deep breathing would help. Or a bath?

WENDY.   You made every girl like me think maybe it's all right to be ourselves.

BETTE.   And that's bad?

WENDY.   It's really confusing.

BETTE.   Would you like to lie down?

WENDY.   Yes.

BETTE.   Just curl up on the couch. You'll feel better soon. Maybe it was all that traffic. I'll sing you a lullaby. *(Bette begins to sing "The Rose."\* Wendy falls asleep.)*

## SCENE THREE

*Bette Midler's dining room table.*

BETTE.   Better?

WENDY.   Much better.

BETTE.   Your eyes are wandering all around the room. Do you want me to give you a tour of my apartment?

WENDY.   No, that's fine. I just have an eye that goes out slightly.

BETTE.   Oh, there I was thinking you were bored and really it's an affliction.

WENDY.   I'm sorry.

BETTE.   Please stop apologizing.

WENDY.   There's nothing wrong with my eyes. I'm just curious. That's all.

BETTE.   Because you'd like to make some quick assessments.

WENDY.   Something like a chinchilla couch would be helpful. Mention Bette Midler and the expectation is outrageous.

BETTE.   Does my domesticity bore you?

\* See Special Note on Songs and Recordings on copyright page.

WENDY.   No, but in truth, you just seem like everyone else. A successful working woman.

BETTE.   These days I am trying to be a little more relaxed about work. I was never meaner to anyone than myself. Now I hope I'm past that. Now I hope I've grown up a little and have given up the angst. Do you mind if I change out of the half-shell outfit into overalls and a T-shirt? I actually like to be in comfortable clothes.

WENDY.   But that's so normal!

BETTE.   I know. I'm disappointingly normal. Frankly, my daughter was the best change in my life. Does that sound too much like everyone else? Because for me it's very special. Are you married?

WENDY.   No.

BETTE.   I thought you were. It's hard work but worth it.

WENDY.   I've been thinking that.

BETTE.   And you look great. I like your hair. I say the older you get the blonder you get.

WENDY.   I think it would be peculiar if I went any blonder.

BETTE.   You're much too self-conscious. You can be anyone you want to be. *(Bette begins to sing "When You Wish upon a Star."\* Wendy is weeping.)*


# SCENE FOUR


*Bette and Wendy together with silvery gum wrappers in their hair at Orbe's Hair Salon.*


BETTE.   People are a lot less original than they used to be. Personalities used to be so much stronger. I find coolness equals dull.

WENDY.   Most people find coolness equals cool.

BETTE.   Boring.

\* See Special Note on Songs and Recordings on copyright page.

10

WENDY.　And withholding equals interesting.

BETTE.　Where are you getting this from? You need to have a better time and wear makeup.

WENDY.　I never wear makeup.

BETTE.　I eat, breathe, and live for makeup.

WENDY.　Why?

BETTE.　It's fun. You should try it.

WENDY.　But other people do it better.

BETTE.　Who cares? Don't you work hard enough in life?

WENDY.　Yes.

BETTE.　So why make the simple things even harder. Just repeat after me, "Anything you can do I can do better."

WENDY.　Anything you can do I can do better. *(Bette sings, "Anything You Can Do I Can Do Better."\* The entire beauty parlor in pink robes joins in the chorus.)*

## SCENE FIVE

*Bette and Wendy at the Saks makeup counter.*

MAKE-UP GIRL.　I think you are one of the greatest women of this century.

BETTE.　I can think of other greater women. Doctors, environmentalists, teachers, dancers. I really admire dancers. They have such discipline.

MAKE-UP GIRL.　But you always make me laugh.

BETTE.　Comedy is very easy for me. When you know what's funny you can be funny. I love to laugh. I find it's therapeutic. I love to laugh till I cry. What do you have in a lip liner?

MAKE-UP GIRL.　I can't believe I'm selling Bette Midler lip liner.

BETTE.　It's for my friend Wendy here. She's scared of makeup.

* See Special Note on Songs and Recordings on copyright page.

11

MAKE-UP GIRL.   That's so sad.

WENDY.   I got frightened by a mascara wand when I was six.

BETTE.   She thinks only one kind of woman deserves to feel attractive.

MAKE-UP GIRL.   That's insane.

BETTE.   I told her that.

MAKE-UP GIRL.   It's no big deal.

BETTE.   I told her that too. There are much more important things in life. When I turned 50 I did a little stock taking and I'm proud of what I've done. Basically, I've done what I set out to do, had fun along the way, and haven't offended too many people. My family is intact. My daughter is a great person so I've been well rewarded. I know you don't get any credit for being happy. But I'm ultimately positive. *(Bette begins to sing "Got the Sun in the Morning and the Moon at Night."\* Wendy buys 100 Topaz lip liners.)*

## SCENE SIX

*Wendy and Bette in a row boat on the Hudson River. It is twilight.*

WENDY.   I love the city at twilight. I can't think of any time that's more romantic.

BETTE.   You're a real New Yorker?

WENDY.   Always. A nice Jewish girl from Brooklyn.

BETTE.   I came to New York at 19 in 1965. I'm a nice Jewish girl from Hawaii.

WENDY.   Not common.

BETTE.   A specialty act. I have always had a sense of not being a Mainlander. And when I got here I didn't have the same experience as everyone else. For instance, I never went to college.

WENDY.   I first heard about you when I was at Yale.

* See Special Note on Songs and Recordings on copyright page.

BETTE.  Miss La-De-Dah.

WENDY.  I was at Drama School. My friends saw you at The Continental Baths.

BETTE.  That was an amazing time.

WENDY.  Over 20 years ago. Most women aren't allowed to stick around for such a long time.

BETTE.  Could you please row instead of talk?

WENDY.  What I mean is you're a survivor.

BETTE.  See that little red light house under the George Washington Bridge. That was cleaned up by "The New York Restoration Project." I was part of that. I take a lot of satisfaction now in the world, surviving. Not just me. Maybe that's what turning 50 is about. Personally, I've never been happier. *(Bette begins to sing "Shine On Harvest Moon."* Wendy harmonizes and rows.)*

## SCENE SEVEN

*The stage at Radio City Music Hall. Wendy rises from the orchestra in a lamé bikini on a half-shell with a blonde wig and six-foot eyelashes.*

WENDY.  And you were expecting The Little Mermaid? I'd like to introduce tonight a woman who has taught us all that a woman can be funny, sexy, warm, 50, a perfectionist, a mother, glitzy, colorful, smart and confident. I am proud to introduce my new best friend Bette Midler. *(The Rockettes tap onstage in Rose-spangled hot pants and Bette simply walks out in overalls and a sweatshirt.)*

BETTE.  I want to thank my new best friend Wendy and I want everyone here to tell her how much they love her lip liner.

ALL OF RADIO CITY.  We love your lip liner Wendy. *(Bette and Wendy sing "Wherever We Go It's Together."*)*

## END OF FANTASY

* See Special Note on Songs and Recordings on copyright page.

# WAITING FOR PHILIP GLASS

INSPIRED BY SHAKESPEARE'S SONNET 94

WAITING FOR PHILIP GLASS was part of an evening entitled *Love's Fire*, seven plays inspired by Shakespeare sonnets written by seven playwrights: Eric Bogosian, Ntozake Shange, Marsha Norman, Tony Kushner, William Finn, John Guare and Wendy Wasserstein. The Acting Company, a national repertory company, Margaret Harley, Producing Director, commissioned them and produced them in association with the Guthrie Theater in Minneapolis and the Barbican Centre in London. The Play premiered at the Guthrie Theater Lab on January 7, 1998. It was directed by Mark Lamos; the set design was by Michael Yeargan; the costume design was by Candice Donnelly; and the lighting design was by Robert Wierzel. The cast was as follows:

HOLDEN .................................................................. Erika Rolfsrud
SPENCER................................................................. Jennifer Rohn
HARRY .................................................................. Stephen DeRosa
LAURA................................................................... Heather Robison
GERRY ...................................................................... James Farmer
RINA.............................................................................. Lisa Tharps
JOE............................................................................. Daniel Pearce

SONNET 94........................................................ Jason Alan Carvell
and Jennifer Rohn

16

# WAITING FOR PHILIP GLASS

### INSPIRED BY SHAKESPEARE'S SONNET 94

*Two women are standing in an East Hampton living room. The room is obviously the home of a contemporary collector. The women are around 35 and extremely attractive. Spencer wears a halter that shoves off her well-sculptured body. Holden wears a softer caftan, looking more ethereal. Spencer is looking at a vase of lilies.*

HOLDEN.   Do you think they're happy in there?

SPENCER.   I've never seen your house look prettier. These flowers are amazing.

HOLDEN.   Ecuadorian lilies. That doesn't mean they're happy in there.

SPENCER.   Why wouldn't they be happy? They're eating. They're talking. And everybody's here.

HOLDEN.   The guest of honor isn't here.

SPENCER.   He'll be here. *(A couple walks by. Harry and Laura walk into the room.)*

HOLDEN.   Hello, Harry! *(They wear matching sweaters over their shoulders. Harry is excessively warm. He hugs both women.)*

HARRY.   I'm so sorry we're late. We just came from Al's little thing for Henry Kissinger. What a great event! You know my wife, Laura Little? Laura, this is our gracious host. *(They shake hands.)*

HOLDEN.   I admire your work. And this is Spencer Blumfeld.

SPENCER.   *(Kisses Laura.)* We know each other. You look so beautiful.

HOLDEN.   Can I get you a drink? Philip Glass will be here any minute.

HARRY. Who's that?

SPENCER. The guest of honor. Tonight is a benefit for him.

LAURA. Harry, he's a very important avant-garde artist. Cutting edge. He directed *Einstein on the Beach*, which I could sit through every night. *(Harry puts his arm around Laura.)*

HARRY. We popped over to Spain last week for the Guggenheim opening in Bilbao. I can't tell you how exciting that little museum is. *(He kisses her.)*

LAURA. I'm training Harry to start thinking globally. It's our job to keep up. *(He kisses her again.)*

HARRY. Everyone thinks I married her for her looks. It's not true, I did it for her energy.

LAURA. Honey, I think I'd like some water.

HARRY. No ice. Lime. *(They walk into the next room.)*

HOLDEN. Robert Wilson.

SPENCER. What?

HOLDEN. She thinks she's here to see Robert Wilson. He directed *Einstein on the Beach*. Our guest is the composer.

SPENCER. She won't know the difference.

HOLDEN. Do you think she's a good writer?

SPENCER. If you think an overrated sex column is good writing.

HOLDEN. Harry's a very nice man but ...

SPENCER. But you could never marry him. Not even just for five years to fulfill the prenup? 'Cause she'll be leaving him the day after. That's not a diamond on her finger. It's a satellite dish.

HOLDEN. I'd do anything for this night to be over.

SPENCER. You can't be cuckoo enough to think they were madly in love.

HOLDEN. Why not? It would have been nice.

SPENCER. But highly unlikely.

HOLDEN. I'm just not up for this. I look enormous and ancient.

SPENCER. I think you look great. But if you're unhappy, I'm thrilled with my eyelift.

HOLDEN. You look fabulous.

SPENCER. Our health and beauty department has done the

research. When a woman turns 35 it's blastoff for corrective surgery. Any later you lose the skin's elasticity. I'm giving you great advice and you're not listening to me.

HOLDEN.   I just wish he would goddamn get here.

SPENCER.   Who? Have you invited someone else I should know about?

HOLDEN.   No. The guest of honor. The artist in question. And I wish everyone hadn't just seen each other at Alan's perfect little thing for Henry Kissinger. And furthermore, where the fuck is Diane Sawyer?

SPENCER.   Take it easy. I thought you said that shrink of yours is helping you.

HOLDEN.   She's helping me with the memory of my mother who lowered my self-esteem by competing with me for attention from my withholding father. That has nothing to do at all with this evening being done and over.

SPENCER.   I give up. I really don't know what you want.

HOLDEN.   I want Diane Sawyer here. And I want Philip Glass here. *(A balding man of around 35 comes into the room. He is not conventionally attractive but commands attention. He is compulsively eating crudités.)*

GERRY.   You changed caterers. I hate caviar in baby bliss potatoes. Give me a cocktail frank or Swedish meatball any day. How are you, Spencer?

SPENCER.   I'm terrific, Gerry. Congratulations on your marriage. I met your wife's dad in Washington the other day.

GERRY.   Are you spending a lot of time with the Secretary of Transportation?

SPENCER.   It was a party at Ben Bradlee's and Sally Quinn's for our September issue.

GERRY.   Well you certainly caused a nice little buzz with that.

SPENCER.   Thank you. I didn't know you read women's magazines.

GERRY.   I read everything. But you should do more about emerging Hollywood. No one cares about Michelle Pfeiffer and her babies anymore.

SPENCER.  Holden, can I get you another spritzer?

HOLDEN.  I'm fine. Thanks.

GERRY.  Honey, she just wants an excuse to run and tell everyone she can't believe what I just said to her.

SPENCER.  I'll bring you back a Swedish meatball. *(Spencer leaves the room.)*

GERRY.  I've never understood your interest in that woman. She's a hideous climber and eveyone says she's going to be fired. That September issue was a total embarrassment. And the entire company's up for sale anyway.

HOLDEN.  Are you buying it?

GERRY.  Boring. It's no fun if it's just about making money. I'd rather stay home with my wife. You're looking well.

HOLDEN.  Thank you.

GERRY.  Kids are good?

HOLDEN.  Kids are great. Kip's in Maine and Taylor's at this terrific summer camp in Cambodia. She's learning to plant rice and dig her own latrine.

GERRY.  So you won't have to tip the doorman at 873 Park Avenue to do it anymore.

HOLDEN.  That was an easy shot.

GERRY.  You set it up.

HOLDEN.  I read you bought that English publishing house.

GERRY.  Now this is seriously interesting. You buy the world's largest chain of discount drugstores and nobody notices. You buy Jonathan Swift's bankrupt publishing house and Henry Kissinger's congratulating you. By the way, you should have come to Alan's little thing for him.

HOLDEN.  Well I was here. Organizing my own little thing.

GERRY.  I'd say it was the classiest event of the summer. The regulars like Mike and Diane Sawyer were there but there were some neat surprises, too.

HOLDEN.  Diane Sawyer was there?

GERRY.  And Bill Bradley, Steven Spielberg, April Gornick, and Erik Fischl.

HOLDEN.  The painters?

GERRY. Alan is considered a major collector now. Rina and I ran into him at the Guggenheim opening in Bilbao. You have got to get there. You know I never thought much of Gehry's work but he has really hit his stride. But if I had to do it all over again I'd be an architect.

HOLDEN. Then you'd have to listen to other people's opinions.

GERRY. I'd hate that.

HOLDEN. I know.

GERRY. A lot of your friends were there and Harry and the sexpert. She should be sued for malpractice for those columns. I've tried those positions and they're only possible for a spastic giraffe or a lesbian hydra.

HOLDEN. Gerry, shh. They're here.

GERRY. Why do you let these kinds of people into your house?

HOLDEN. He's a friend of mine.

GERRY. She's an ex-lover of mine. That doesn't mean I have to feed her. I have to say I was very lucky. After my first marriage there was basically you and Rina. You two were the standouts.

HOLDEN. Well, at least we had the most quotable fathers. So you liked Bilbao?

GERRY. You really don't want to talk about us. Or why until tonight you've avoided meeting my new wife.

HOLDEN. I'm just waiting for Philip Glass.

GERRY. Why don't you tell your guests if they write a check they can all go home now. All they want is to be excused. We all just saw each other with Henry Kissinger anyhow.

HOLDEN. You don't have to stay, Gerry ...

GERRY. I have to stay, I'm only here for you. *(Kisses her.)* Where's that guy you've been dating?

HOLDEN. He's inside.

GERRY. I heard he's a something.

HOLDEN. Developer.

GERRY. Sounds promising. What does he develop?

HOLDEN. Pennsylvania.

GERRY. You can do better.

HOLDEN.  What's the matter with Pennsylvania?

GERRY.  Nothing. Except Liberty Bell condos.

HOLDEN.  How do you know the name of his condos?

GERRY.  I pay attention. That's my business. Holden, you don't need to throw it all away on some dolt who drives a Lexus. Does he wear Gucci loafers? 'Cause it would kill me to see you with a guy in Gucci loafers. At least wait till you're 40.

HOLDEN.  He wears Hermès loafers.

GERRY.  Are you doing this deliberately? *(Rina, a beautiful young woman of around 22 comes into the room. She is dressed in something resembling a slip.)* There you are. We were just talking about you. *(He kisses her.)*

RINA.  This is such a beautiful house.

GERRY.  I think it's one of Bobby Stern's better ones. Delightful play of air and light. Holden's father had it built.

HOLDEN.  It was kind of a first wedding present.

GERRY.  Holden's father was a philosophy professor at Princeton. Wonderful man. Sort of my idol.

HOLDEN.  He was alcoholic and married five times before his suicide.

GERRY.  But he spent his life paying attention to what truly interested him. Of course I have no robber barons in my family so that was never an option for me.

RINA.  These are beautiful lilies. Where are the from?

HOLDEN.  Ecuador. They're much heartier than the ones from Holland.

GERRY.  Holden does her own flowers.

HOLDEN.  It's a hobby of mine. My daughter asked me once why I hired a man to put flowers into a vase. *(They all laugh uncomfortably. A burly man in a Gucci belt and loafers comes into the room.)*

JOE.  So where's the guest of honor?

HOLDEN.  He's on his way. Joe, I don't think you know my friend Gerry Gavshon.

JOE.  No, but of course I'm always reading about you. Congratulations on that Binmart deal. You're killing every discount store in my part of the country.

GERRY. We're opening next month in Moscow and Beijing. Who knew that in our lifetime we could say we made the world safe for Alka-Seltzer. This is my wife, Rina. Are you a big fan of Philip Glass?

JOE. Holden took me to see something of his.

HOLDEN. *Glass Pieces.* The Jerome Robbins ballet.

JOE. The one with those gorgeous young people going across the stage.

GERRY. That could be a lot of things.

HOLDEN. No, Joe, you're right. I know the one you mean.

JOE. Personally, I like a song that goes somewhere. But you've got to give them both credit. It was a lively show and most of the time ballet except for the jumpers can be really boring.

HOLDEN. Do you go to the ballet, Rina?

GERRY. We prefer the opera. We're going practically every free evening. I used to be intimidated but it's really very easy to pick up.

JOE. That's the way to stay young. Learn something new. Have you ever been on an Outward Bound trip?

GERRY. Spending the night alone on a mountain in Colorado? I'm from the suburbs of Pittsburgh, Joe. I know the answer. I'd never survive without take-out Chinese.

JOE. You eat a few roots and you're fine. Listen, I've been with them on Hurricane Island, I've sailed a Viking ship down a fjord, but last week I did something extraordinary. I went solo to the South Bronx for a night. Terrible neighborhood. Crack vials on the street. People you think if you look them in the face you'll never see your kids again. And I made it through. First time I've been really scared in years.

RINA. Once the baby's born I want to teach cooking at a Phoenix House in the South Bronx.

GERRY. Sweetie, they don't need to learn fat-free cooking at a Phoenix House in the South Bronx.

HOLDEN. When is your baby due?

RINA. Next March. Gerry wants a large family. I told him now that we've got the ranch even six kids is okay with me.

HOLDEN. What ranch?

23

GERRY. We got a little place in Jackson Hole. Around one thousand acres. And it's easy to get to if you don't rely on commercial airlines. We just pop over to Teterboro and we're there. Believe me it makes a lot more sense than driving to the Berkshires. *(Spencer comes back into the room.)*

SPENCER. Honey, people are beginning to start leaving. Nora told me to give you a big kiss but she had to meet Diane Sawyer, and Kathleen Turner says she had to rush out before her babysitter turned psycho. *(Harry and Laura come out.)*

HARRY. We heard he wasn't coming.

HOLDEN. He's on his way.

HARRY. Honey, we're expected for dinner.

GERRY. Whose dinner?

HARRY. Just Joe and Patty. Are you going?

GERRY. He's a second-rate talent. With a gift for schmoozing. And she's lucky she hasn't been indicted.

LAURA. I thought they were friends of yours.

HARRY. You two know each other?

GERRY. We're acquainted. Nice seeing you again.

LAURA. Nice seeing you again. It was a great party, Holden. Please tell Mr. Glass I'm one of his greatest fans.

GERRY. Laura ...

LAURA. Yes.

GERRY. I really enjoyed your last column.

LAURA. Thank you. Good night. *(They exit.)*

JOE. What does she write about?

GERRY. Blow jobs.

JOE. That takes guts.

SPENCER. She can't help herself.

HOLDEN. I better go in there and tell them he's on his way.

JOE. Maybe we should invite everyone out for dinner. Nothing wrong with having lobster and white wine overlooking the ocean.

SPENCER. And we could all reenact *Einstein on the Beach.*

HOLDEN. You go ahead.

JOE. What?

HOLDEN. You go ahead. I can't leave my guests.

JOE.  I wouldn't leave you at your party.

HOLDEN.  No, please, take Spencer and get a lobster on the beach.

SPENCER.  What are you talking about?

HOLDEN.  I prefer that you go.

SPENCER.  Gerry, this is your fault.

GERRY.  I didn't say a word.

SPENCER.  Why did you come here?

GERRY.  I was invited. I wanted my old friend to meet my wife.

HOLDEN.  Rina and Gerry bought a ranch where they're hoping to raise a family.

GERRY.  You're not giving Rina the credit she's due. Rina graduated phi Beta Kappa from Bowdoin. She got into Harvard Medical School.

RINA.  Gerry, you don't have to tell everyone that.

GERRY.  Why not? It happens to be true. And Rina's setting up the Rina and Gerry Gavshon Pediatrics Foundation.

RINA.  I think I would like to go home now. I'm feeling a little tired.

GERRY.  We can't leave now.

RINA.  Would you drop me at home?

JOE.  Of course.

GERRY.  What are you doing?

RINA.  My feet are hurting. I need to lie down.

GERRY.  You can lie down here until the guest of honor comes.

JOE.  Spencer and I will take you home.

HOLDEN.  You're a gentleman, Joe.

JOE.  I'll just drop her off and be right back.

HOLDEN.  You don't have to.

SPENCER.  Are you insane?

HOLDEN.  No. I'm waiting for Philip Glass. *(She kisses Spencer on the cheek.)* Good night.

GERRY.  You just sent a perfectly nice man away.

HOLDEN.  I thought I shouldn't throw myself away on a dolt who drives a Lexus.

GERRY.  You shouldn't listen so carefully to everything I say.

HOLDEN.   Your wife is charming. I liked her a lot.

GERRY.   She gets tired. But when you total it all up she makes the most sense.

HOLDEN.   A good long-term investment.

GERRY.   Don't be crude.

HOLDEN.   I didn't get to Bilbao. I am crude. Would you excuse me while I retrieve my party? *(He grabs her by the arm.)*

GERRY.   What the hell is wrong with you?

HOLDEN.   Nothing. I just want to tell them to wait. That's all.

GERRY.   It makes no difference if they wait.

HOLDEN.   But our guest will come and tell us all what it's like to be an artist. What it's like to think you can make up a life that's different from your own.

GERRY.   There's nothing wrong with your life.

HOLDEN.   You're absolutely right there's nothing wrong with it at all.

GERRY.   Let me take you to dinner tonight? After he leaves.

HOLDEN.   I can't. I have a date.

GERRY.   Your date just left.

HOLDEN.   He's not my only date.

GERRY.   So you're leaving me here alone.

HOLDEN.   Good for me. Bad for you. Isn't that what you once told me in business had to be true.

GERRY.   This isn't business. This is friendship.

HOLDEN.   I'm tired of friendship. Good night, Gerry. *(She kisses Gerry.)* Thank you so much for dropping by.

GERRY.   You have no idea how much I respect you.

HOLDEN.   It's great news about Binmart in Moscow!

GERRY.   *(Suddenly yells.)* Talk to me, Holden! *(She takes the lilies out of the vase.)*

HOLDEN.   These are for Rina.

GERRY.   Please, you don't have to.

HOLDEN.   Most likely I won't be here in the morning. And lilies that fester smell far worse than weeds. Good night. *(She watches as Gerry leaves the room. Holden stands up, pulls herself up straight, and walks into the adjoining room.)* Everyone. He's on his way.

**END**

# SONNET 94

They that have pow'r to hurt and will do none,
That do not do the thing they most do show,
Who, moving others, are themselves as stone,
Unmoved, cold, and to temptation slow —
They rightly do inherit heaven's graces,
And husband Nature's riches from expense;
They are the lords and owners of their faces,
Others but stewards of their excellence.
The summer's flow'r is to the summer sweet,
Though to itself it only live and die;
But if that flow'r with base infection meet,
The basest weed outbraves his dignity:
   For sweetest things turn sourest by their deeds;
   Lilies that fester smell far worse than weeds.

# TENDER OFFER

TENDER OFFER was produced by The Ensemble Studio Theatre at the Annual Festival of One-Act Plays Marathon 1983. It was directed by Jerry Zaks; the set design was by Johniene Papandreas; the lighting design was by Geoffrey Dunbar; the sound design was by Bruce Ellman; the costume design was by Deborah Shaw; the stage manager was Nancy Rifkind; the production manager was Teresa Elwert; and the production stage manager was Richard Costabile. The cast was as follows:

LISA ............................................................. Alyssa Milano
PAUL ........................................................ James Eckhouse

# TENDER OFFER

*Lisa is alone in a dance studio. She is nine, dressed in traditional leotards and tights. She begins singing to herself, "Nothing Could Be Finer Than to Be in Carolina." She maps out a dance routine, including parts for the chorus. She builds to a finale. A man, Paul, around 35, walks in. He has a sweet, though distant, demeanor. As he walks in, Lisa notices him and stops.*

PAUL.   You don't have to stop, sweetheart.

LISA.   That's okay.

PAUL.   Looked very good.

LISA.   Thanks.

PAUL.   Don't I get a kiss hello?

LISA.   Sure.

PAUL.   *(Embraces her.)* Hi, Tiger.

LISA.   Hi, Dad.

PAUL.   I'm sorry I'm late.

LISA.   That's okay.

PAUL.   How'd it go?

LISA.   Good.

PAUL.   Just good?

LISA.   Pretty good.

PAUL.   "Pretty good." You mean you got a lot of applause or "pretty good" you could have done better.

LISA.   Well, Courtney Palumbo's mother thought I was pretty good. But you know the part in the middle when everybody's supposed to freeze and the big girl comes out. Well, I think I moved a little bit.

PAUL.   I thought what you were doing looked very good.

LISA.   Daddy, that's not what I was doing. That was tap-dancing. I made that up.

PAUL. Oh. Well it looked good. Kind of sexy.

LISA. Yuch!

PAUL. What do you mean "yuch"?

LISA. Just yuch!

PAUL. You don't want to be sexy?

LISA. I don't care.

PAUL. Let's go, Tiger. I promised your mother I'd get you home in time for dinner.

LISA. I can't find my leg warmers.

PAUL. You can't find your what?

LISA. Leg warmers. I can't go home till I find my leg warmers.

PAUL. I don't see you looking for them.

LISA. I was waiting for you.

PAUL. Oh.

LISA. Daddy.

PAUL. What?

LISA. Nothing.

PAUL. Where do you think you left them?

LISA. Somewhere around here. I can't remember.

PAUL. Well, try to remember, Lisa. We don't have all night.

LISA. I told you. I think somewhere around here.

PAUL. I don't see them. Let's go home now. You'll call the dancing school tomorrow.

LISA. Daddy, I can't go home till I find them. Miss Judy says it's not professional to leave things.

PAUL. Who's Miss Judy?

LISA. She's my ballet teacher. She once danced the lead in *Swan Lake,* and she was a June Taylor dancer.

PAUL. Well, then, I'm sure she'll understand about the leg warmers.

LISA. Daddy, Miss Judy wanted to know why you were late today.

PAUL. Hmmmmmmmm?

LISA. Why were you late?

PAUL. I was in a meeting. Business. I'm sorry.

LISA. Why did you tell Mommy you'd come instead of her if you knew you had business?

PAUL. Honey, something just came up. I thought I'd be able to be here. I was looking forward to it.

LISA. I wish you wouldn't make appointments to see me.

PAUL. Hmmmmmmmm.

LISA. You shouldn't make appointments to see me unless you know you're going to come.

PAUL. Of course I'm going to come.

LISA. No, you're not. Talia Robbins told me she's much happier living without her father in the house. Her father used to come home late and go to sleep early.

PAUL. Lisa, stop it. Let's go.

LISA. I can't find my leg warmers.

PAUL. Forget your leg warmers.

LISA. Daddy.

PAUL. What is it?

LISA. I saw this show on television, I think it was WPIX Channel 11. Well, the father was crying about his daughter.

PAUL. Why was he crying? Was she sick?

LISA. No. She was at school. And he was at business. And he just missed her, so he started to cry.

PAUL. What was the name of this show?

LISA. I don't know. I came in in the middle.

PAUL. Well, Lisa, I certainly would cry if you were sick or far away, but I know that you're well and you're home. So no reason to get maudlin.

LISA. What's maudlin?

PAUL. Sentimental, soppy. Frequently used by children who make things up to get attention.

LISA. I am sick! I am sick! I have Hodgkin's disease and a bad itch on my leg.

PAUL. What do you mean you have Hodgkin's disease? Don't say things like that.

LISA. Swoosie Kurtz, she had Hodgkin's disease on a TV movie last year, but she got better and now she's on *Love Sidney*.

PAUL. Who is Swoosie Kurtz?

LISA. She's an actress named after an airplane. I saw her on *Live at Five*.

PAUL. You watch too much television; you should do your homework. Now, put your coat on.

LISA. Daddy, I really do have a bad itch on my leg. Would you scratch it?

PAUL. Lisa, you're procrastinating.

LISA. Why do you use words I don't understand? I hate it. You're like Daria Feldman's mother. She always talks in Yiddish to her husband so Daria won't understand.

PAUL. Procrastinating is not Yiddish.

LISA. Well, I don't know what it is.

PAUL. Procrastinating means you don't want to go about your business.

LISA. I don't go to business. I go to school.

PAUL. What I mean is you want to hang around here until you and I are late for dinner and your mother's angry and it's too late for you to do your homework.

LISA. I do not.

PAUL. Well, it sure looks that way. Now put your coat on and let's go.

LISA. Daddy.

PAUL. Honey, I'm tired. Really, later.

LISA. Why don't you want to talk to me?

PAUL. I do want to talk to you. I promise when we get home we'll have a nice talk.

LISA. No, we won't. You'll read the paper and fall asleep in front of the news.

PAUL. Honey, we'll talk on the weekend, I promise. Aren't I taking you to the theater this weekend? Let me look. *(He takes out appointment book.)* Yes. Sunday. *Joseph and the Amazing Technicolor Raincoat* with Lisa. Okay, Tiger?

LISA. Sure. It's Dreamcoat.

PAUL. What?

LISA. Nothing. I think I see my leg warmers. *(She goes to pick them up, and an odd-looking trophy.)*

PAUL. What's that?

LISA. It's stupid. I was second best at the dance recital, so they gave me this thing. It's stupid.

PAUL. Lisa.

LISA. What?

PAUL. What did you want to talk about?

LISA. Nothing.

PAUL. Was it about my missing your recital? I'm really sorry, Tiger. I would have liked to have been here.

LISA. That's okay.

PAUL. Honest?

LISA. Daddy, you're prostrastinating.

PAUL. I'm procrastinating. Sit down. Let's talk. So. How's school?

LISA. Fine.

PAUL. You like it?

LISA. Yup.

PAUL. You looking forward to camp this summer?

LISA. Yup.

PAUL. Is Daria Feldman going back?

LISA. Nope.

PAUL. Why not?

LISA. I don't know. We can go home now. Honest, my foot doesn't itch anymore.

PAUL. Lisa, you know what you do in business when it seems like there's nothing left to say? That's when you really start talking. Put a bid on the table.

LISA. What's a bid?

PAUL. You tell me what you want and I'll tell you what I've got to offer. Like Monopoly. You want Boardwalk, but I'm only willing to give you the Railroads. Now, because you are my daughter I'd throw in Water Works and Electricity. Understand, Tiger?

LISA. No. I don't like board games. You know, Daddy, we could get Space Invaders for our home for 35 dollars. In fact, we could get an Osborne System for two thousand. Daria Feldman's parents ...

PAUL. Daria Feldman's parents refuse to talk to Daria, so they bought a computer to keep Daria busy so they won't have to speak in Yiddish. Daria will probably grow up to be a homicidal maniac lesbian prostitute.

LISA.    I know what that word prostitute means.

PAUL.    Good. *(Pause.)* You still haven't told me about school. Do you still like your teacher?

LISA.    She's okay.

PAUL.    Lisa, if we're talking try to answer me.

LISA.    I am answering you. Can we go home now, please?

PAUL.    Damn it, Lisa, if you want to talk to me ... Talk to me!

LISA.    I can't wait till I'm old enough so I can make my own money and never have to see you again. Maybe I'll become a prostitute.

PAUL.    Young lady, that's enough.

LISA.    I hate you, Daddy! I hate you! *(She throws her trophy into the trash bin.)*

PAUL.    What'd you do that for?

LISA.    It's stupid.

PAUL.    Maybe I wanted it.

LISA.    What for?

PAUL.    Maybe I wanted to put it where I keep your dinosaur and the picture you made of Mrs. Kimbel with the chicken pox.

LISA.    You got mad at me when I made that picture. You told me I had to respect Mrs. Kimbel because she was my teacher.

PAUL.    That's true. But she wasn't my teacher. I liked her better with the chicken pox. *(Pause.)* Lisa, I'm sorry. I was very wrong to miss your recital, and you don't have to become a prostitute. That's not the type of profession Miss Judy has in mind for you.

LISA.    *(Mumbles.)* No.

PAUL.    No. *(Pause.)* So Talia Robbins is really happy her father moved out?

LISA.    Talia Robbins picks open the eight-grade lockers during gym period. But she did that before her father moved out.

PAUL.    You can't always judge someone by what they do or what they don't do. Sometimes you come home from dancing school and run upstairs and shut the door, and when I finally get to talk to you, everything is "okay" or "fine." Yup or nope?

LISA.    Yup.

PAUL.   Sometimes, a lot of times, I come home and fall asleep in front of the television. So you and I spend a lot of time being a little scared of each other. Maybe?

LISA.   Maybe.

PAUL.   Tell you what. I'll make you a tender offer.

LISA.   What?

PAUL.   I'll make you a tender offer. That's when one company publishes in the newspaper that they want to buy another company. And the company that publishes is called the Black Knight because they want to gobble up the poor little company. So the poor little company needs to be rescued. And then a White Knight comes along and makes a bigger and better offer so the shareholders won't have to tender shares to the Big Black Knight. You with me?

LISA.   Sort of.

PAUL.   I'll make you a tender offer like the White Knight. But I don't want to own you. I just want to make a much better offer. Okay?

LISA.   *(Sort of understanding.)* Okay. *(Pause. They sit for a moment.)* Sort of, Daddy, what do you think about? I mean, like when you're quiet what do you think about?

PAUL.   Oh, business usually. If I think I made a mistake or if I think I'm doing okay. Sometimes I think about what I'll be doing five years from now and if it's what I hoped it would be five years ago. Sometimes I think about what your life will be like, if Mount Saint Helen's will erupt again. What you'll become if you'll study penmanship or word processing. If you speak kindly of me to your psychiatrist when you are in graduate school. And how the hell I'll pay for your graduate school. And sometimes I try and think what it was I thought about when I was your age.

LISA.   Do you ever look out your window at the clouds and try to see which kinds of shapes they are? Like one time, honest, I saw the head of Walter Cronkite in a flower vase. Really! Like look don't those kinda look like if you turn it upside down, two big elbows or two elephant trunks dancing?

PAUL.   Actually still looks like Walter Cronkite in a flower vase to me. But look up a little. See the one that's still moving? That sorta looks like a whale on a thimble.

LISA.   Where?

PAUL.   Look up. To your right.

LISA.   I don't see it. Where?

PAUL.   The other way.

LISA.   Oh, yeah! There's the head and there's the stomach. Yeah! *(Lisa picks up her trophy.)* Hey, Daddy.

PAUL.   Hey, Lisa.

LISA.   You can have this thing if you want it. But you have to put it like this, because if you put it like that it is gross.

PAUL.   You know what I'd like? So I can tell people who come into my office why I have this gross stupid thing on my shelf, I'd like it if you could show me your dance recital.

LISA.   Now?

PAUL.   We've got time. Mother said she won't be home till late.

LISA.   Well, Daddy, during a lot of it I freeze and the big girl in front dances.

PAUL.   Well, how 'bout the number you were doing when I walked in?

LISA.   Well, see, I have parts for a lot of people in that one, too.

PAUL.   I'll dance the other parts.

LISA.   You can't dance.

PAUL.   Young lady, I played Yvette Mimimeux in a Hasty Pudding Show.

LISA.   Who's Yvette Mimimeux?

PAUL.   Watch more television. You'll find out. *(Paul stands up.)* So I'm ready. *(He begins singing.)* "Nothing could be finer than to be in Carolina."

LISA.   Now I go. "In the morning." And now you go. Dum-da.

PAUL.   *(Obviously not a tap dancer.)* Da-da-dum.

LISA.   *(Whines.)* Daddy!

PAUL.   *(Mimics her.)* Lisa! "Nothing could be finer ... "

LISA.   That looks dumb.

PAUL.   Oh, yeah? You think they do this better in *The Amazing Minkcoat*? No way! Now you go — da da da dum.

LISA.   Da da da dum.

PAUL.   "If I had Aladdin's lamp for only a day, I'd make a wish ... "

LISA.   Daddy, that's maudlin!

PAUL.   I know it's maudlin. And here's what I'd say:

LISA AND PAUL.   I'd say that "nothing could be finer than to be in Carolina in the mooooooooooornin'."

# WORKOUT

# WORKOUT

*A woman enters a small room wearing leotards and a midi sweat top. She turns on disco music and lies on the floor. She begins to exercise, and begins to talk.*

Ready for your workout? We'll start with buttock tucks. These are my favorite. Now lie back, breathe deep. Big breath. Mmmmmm. Relax, feet forward. Remember, make the muscles burn. *(She begins to bounce her buttocks.)*

And lift and lower. And lift and lower. Squeeze it. Squeeze it. Push up, release. Push up and release. Really squeeze it, Denise. Lift up, lift up and bounce bounce bounce. *(She begins doing leg lifts.)*

This is what I like to think about when I'm doing my workout. I think about how I got up at four-thirty in the morning and ran for five miles. And how great that run felt. Keep bouncing, up down up down. I like to think about the brewer's yeast I gave my children for breakfast. Squeeze it! Squeeze it! And how proud I am that the words "french toast" are never used in our house. I think about my husband's stamina. It's better now than when we first got married because we're organized. Work deep. Work deep! *(She does lifts in fire hydrant position.)*

And I think about the novel I'm writing between nine and eleven this morning. And the chain of appliance stores I'm opening at twelve. I just think it's so important that we take charge of our own appliances. Last week I restored the electricity for the city of Fresno. And a year ago I couldn't use a can opener. Just keep bouncing, Denise. And one, and two. And this afternoon after my yoghurt shake ... *(She goes into a split.)*

Oooooooooooooh I felt the burn that time. I'm going to learn ancient Egyptian so I can star in the Nefertiti story, which I am also producing, directing, writing, editing, and distributing. I'll need all my strength. Let's do twenty more. Denise, put the gun down. Your life isn't my fault! Be angry with your buttocks. Let them know your feelings. *(She squats, elbow to knee.)*

At five o'clock I'm going to my daughter's dance recital, where my husband will announce his candidacy for governor — I hope you all will vote for him — and I will announce the publication of my new workout book for children under six and their pets. On our way home, the entire family will stop at the home of a woman friend of mine for women's friendship and Tofutti ice cream. Release, release, we're almost there. Don't give in. Push it. Push it. *(She begins doing jumping jacks.)*

And then my very favorite part of the day. Tuck in. Feel it all over. The children are outside playing nonviolent baseball with radishes and zucchinis, my husband is preparing his part of the family meal and debating with Connie Chung and the six o'clock news team by satellite. Just two more. Get ready to release. And it is time for my moment. Just me. *(She stops exercising for the first time.)*

And I sit for the first time in the day. On my favorite chair, with my favorite quilt. And I take a deep breath, and I cry. *(She pauses.)* But just a little. *(She stands up.)*

And then I tuck in my stomach and pull up from the chair. Vertebra by vertebra. And I take a deep inhalation and exhale. And now we're ready for fifty more jumping jacks. And one, and two, and three, let's go, Denise. *(She continues jumping happily.)*

**END**

# MEDEA

## (CO-AUTHORED WITH CHRISTOPHER DURANG)

# MEDEA

*The actress who is to play Medea comes out and makes the following introduction.*

ACTRESS. Hello. I am she who will be Medea. That is, I shall play the heroine from that famous Greek tragedy by Euripides for you.

I attended a first rate School of Dramatic Arts. At this wonderful school, I had classical training, which means we start at the very beginning, a very good place to start. Greek tragedy. How many of you in the audience have ever acted in Greek tragedy? How many of your lives are Greek tragedy? Is Olympia Dukakis here this evening?

As an actress who studied the classics, one of the first things you learn in drama school is that there are more roles for men than for women. This is a wonderful thing to learn because it is true of the real world as well. Except for *Thelma and Louise*. At drama school, in order to compensate for this problem, the women every year got to act in either *The Trojan Women* or *The House of Bernarda Alba*. This prepared us for bit parts on *Designing Women* and *Little House on the Prairie*. Although these shows are cancelled now, and we have nothing to do.

Tonight, we would like to present to you a selection from one of the most famous Greek tragedies ever written, *The Trojan Women*. Our scene is directed by Michael Cacoyannis and choreographed by June Taylor. And now, translated from the Greek by George Stephanoulous, here is a scene from the terrifying tragedy. *(Names the cast members:)* (N) _____, (N) _____ and (N) _____ will play the Chorus. (N) _____ and (N) _____ will play the men. *(Dramatically.)*

And I, (N) _____, will play Medea. *(The actress playing Medea exits with purpose and panache. Enter the three actresses who play the Chorus. They are dressed in togas. Most of the time they speak in unison. Sometimes they speak solo lines. In the style of the piece, they are over-dramatic and over-wrought. But most of the time they should act their lines as if they are the words from genuine Greek tragedy, full of intonation and emotional feeling. Don't send them up, or wink at the audience. Let the juxtaposition of Greek tragedy acting style and the sometimes silly lines be what creates the humor.)*

CHORUS. *(In unison.)*

So pitiful, so pitiful

your shame and lamentation.

No more shall I move the shifting pace

of the shuttle at the looms of Ida.

CHORUS MEMBER #3. *(Echoes.)*

Looms of Ida.

CHORUS.

Can you not, Queen Hecuba, stop this Bacchanal before

her light feet whirl her away into the Argive camp?

CHORUS MEMBER #3. *(Echoes.)*

Argive camp.

CHORUS. *(In unison.)*

O woe, o woe, o woe,

We are so upset we speak in unison,

So pitiful, so wretched, so doomed,

Women who run with wolves

Women who love too much,

Whitewater rapids, how did she turn $1000 into $100,000?

O woe, o woe, o woe.

Here she comes now.

Wooga, wooga, wooga.

*(Enter Medea in a dramatic, blood red toga. She is in high, excessive grief and fury.)*

MEDEA.

Come, flame of the sky,

Pierce through my head!

What do I, Medea, gain from living any longer?

Oh I hate living! I want

to end my life, leave it behind, and die.

CHORUS. *(In unison; chanted seriously.)*
But tell us how you're really feeling.
MEDEA. My husband Jason — the Argonaut — has left me for another woman. Debbie.
CHORUS. *(In unison.)*
Dreaded Debbie, dreaded Debbie.
Debutante from hell.
MEDEA. She is the daughter of King Creon, who owns a diner on 55th Street and Jamaica Avenue. Fie on her! And the House of Creon! And the four brothers of the Acropolis.
I am banished from my husband's bed, and from the country. A bad predicament all around. But I am skilled in poison. Today three of my enemies I will strike down dead: Debbie and Debbie's father and my husband.
CHORUS. *(In unison.)*
Speaking of your husband, here he comes.
*(Enter Jason, dressed in a toga, but also with an armored breast plate and wearing a soldier's helmet with a nice little red adornment on top. Sort of like a costume from either* Ben Hur *or* Cleopatra. *He perhaps is not in the grand style, but sounds more normal and conversational.)*
JASON. Hello, Medea.
MEDEA. Hello, Jason.
JASON. I hear you've been banished to China.
MEDEA. *(Suddenly Noel Coward brittle.)* Very large, China.
JASON. And Japan?
MEDEA. Very small, Japan. And Debbie?
JASON. She's very striking.
MEDEA. Some women should be struck regularly like gongs.
JASON. Medea, even though thou art banished by Creon to foreign shores, the two innocent children of our loins, Lyle and Erik, should remain with me. I will enroll them at the Dalton School. And there they will flourish as citizens of Corinth under the watchful eye of Zeus and his lovely and talented wife Hera.
MEDEA. Fine, walk on me some more! I was born unlucky and a woman.

CHORUS.  *(In unison.)*
Men are from Mars, women are from Venus.
JASON.   Well, whatever. I call the gods to witness that I have done my best to help you and the children.
MEDEA.   Go! You have spent too long out here. You are consumed with craving for your newly-won bride, Debbie. Go, enjoy Debbie! *(Jason shrugs, exits.)* O woe, o woe. I am in pain for I know what I must do. Debbie, kill for sure.
CHORUS.  *(In unison.)*
Debbie's done, ding dong. Debbie's done.
Done deal, Debbie dead.
Dopey Debbie, Debbie dead.
MEDEA.   But also my sons. Never shall their father see them again. I shall kill my children. *(Ferociously, to the Chorus.)* How do you like that????
CHORUS.  *(In unison.)*
Aaaaaaagghghghghghghghgghhhhh!
O smart women, foolish choices.
Stop the insanity! Stop the insanity!
You can eat one slice of cheese, or 16 baked potatoes!
Make up your mind.
MEDEA.   Why is there so little *Trojan Women* in this, and so much of me?
CHORUS.  *(In unison.)*
We don't know *The Trojan Women* as well as we know *Medea.*
*(Spoken, not sung.)*
Medea, we just met a girl named Medea.
And suddenly that name
Will never be the same.
MEDEA.   Bring my children hither.
CHORUS.  *(In unison.)*
O miserable mother, to destroy your own increase, murder the babes of your body. The number you have reached is not in service at this time. Call 777-FILM.
MEDEA.   *(In a boiling fury.)* I want to kill my children. I want to sleep with my brother. I want to pluck out the eyes of my father. I want to blow up the Parthenon. I need a creative outlet for all

this anger. *(Enter the Messenger, carrying a head. He kneels before Medea.)*

MESSENGER.   I am a messenger. Caesar is dead.

CHORUS.   *(In unison.)*

Caesar is dead. How interesting. Who is Caesar?

MESSENGER.   I am sorry. Wrong message. *(Reads from piece of paper.)* Lady Teazle wishes you to know that Lady Windermere and Lady Bracknell are inviting you and Lady The-Scottish-Play to tea with her cousin Ernest, if he's not visiting Mr. Bunberry.

MEDEA.   Mr. Bunberry? I do not need a messenger. I need a deus ex machina. *(Elaborate music. Enter an Angel with great big wings. Descending from the ceiling, or revealed on a balcony. Or dragging a step ladder that he stands on. Very dramatic whatever he does.)*

ANGEL.   O Medea, O Medea.

I am a deus ex machina.

In a bigger production, I would come down from the sky in an angel's outfit, but just use your imagination. Theatre is greatly about imagination, is it not.

I am an angel.

I I I I I I I, yi yi yi.

I I I I am the Bird of Greek Tragedy.

Do not kill your children. Do not sleep with your brother. Rein in your rage, and thank Zeus. I come with glad tidings. Debbie is no more a threat. She's been cast in a series. She has a running part on *Home Improvements.*

CHORUS.   *(In unison.)*

*Home Improvements.*

ANGEL.   Jason will return to you. He sees the error of his ways. He has been lobotomized.

CHORUS.   *(In unison.)*

O fortunate woman, to whom Zeus has awarded a docile husband.

MEDEA.   O, deus ex machina, o, angel:

O, Hecuba, oh, looms of Ida.

CHORUS.   *(In unison.)*

Ida Ida Ida Ida.

MEDEA.   I am eternally grateful to you.

CHORUS. *(In unison.)*

The things we thought would happen do not happen.
The unexpected, God makes possible.

*(Spoken, not sung.)*

The camptown races sing a song,
Do da, do da.

CHORUS AND MEDEA. *(Switch to singing now.)*

Medea's happy the whole day long.
Oh the do da day!
things will be just fine,
Things will just great
No need to kill her children now,
Oh the do da ...

*(Big musical coda:)*

Oh the do da,
Zeus and Buddha,
They're as nice as
Dionysus,
Oh the do da
Work it though da
Oh the do da, do da, do da Day!

*(Medea and the Chorus and the Angel strike a happy and triumphant pose.)*

# BOY MEETS GIRL

NARRATOR. On a spring morning in 1972, a senior at the Spence School was in Central Park, completing her science project on the reproductive cycle of flowering plants, when she saw an unmarked bus drop off twenty women in silk suits, bow ties, and sneakers on the corner of Eighty-ninth Street and Fifth Avenue. The girl took note; when she was in sixth grade, sneakers and suits had been cause for suspension.

Meanwhile, on the West Side, a middle-aged but very nice lady was on her way to Barney Greengrass, the Sturgeon King, on Eighty-ninth Street, when three cars — Volvo, a BMW, and a Saab with M.D. plates and a "Save the Whales" bumper sticker — pulled up to Eighty-seventh Street and Amsterdam Avenue. Fifteen young men, whom the lady thought she recognized from her son's protest days at the University of Wisconsin, emerged from the cars. Before the gracious lady could offer them an Entenmann's cake, they jogged into a dilapidated brownstone and immediately began exposing brick and hanging spider plants.

And the city embraced these pioneers, who were dressed in 100-percent-natural fabric. They prospered and they multiplied. From the now infamous drop-offs grew a new breed of New Yorkers, the Professionalites. Only their ratio of men to women, three to four, has remained constant.

What follows is a Love Story in One Act and Six Scenes between two of these sabra professionalites: Dan and Molly.

# CHARACTERS

MOLLY. 33 years old, single, successful, and quietly desperate. Every Saturday night, Molly sheds her doctorate in molecular microchips and slips into a Zandra Rhodes macromini. On the weekends, Molly is just another girl at The Trading Post, a popular café on the Columbus Avenue strip. Just another S.S.D.B.G. (Single/Successful/Desperate/Bachelor Girl) waiting for a discriminating Root Canal Man to invite her for an unfulfilling weekend at his summer share in the Hamptons. Molly, a native New Yorker, has recently begun considering relocating to the Sun Belt.

DAN. A successful creative director at B.B.D. & O. advertising agency. He is 32, single, and having a ball. Every night, after twelve hours of Clio Award-winning work for his clients, Dan goes to the Odeon, where he eats poached salmon on grilled kiwi fruit at a table crowded with visual artists, conceptual artists, and performing artists. And every night, after picking up the tab, Dan swears that he, too, will one day give up his job and devote himself to art.

DR. SUSAN. Molly's psychiatrist.

STANLEY TANNENBAUM, PH.D. Dan's psychologist.

HER MAJESTY, THE QUEEN. Ruler of the Helmsley Palace.

# BOY MEETS GIRL

## SCENE ONE

*One night in late August, Dan has a yearning to talk to someone who knows Donna Karan but has moved on to Issey Miyake. Dan slips into The Trading Post, where the number of single women is a plague to the West Side zoning committee. It is here that he first sees Molly, seated at the bar. She is young, she is urban, she is professional. He knows immediately that Molly is the kind of new-fashioned girl he could bring home to his analyst's couch. Dan sits next to her.*

DAN.   Hi.

MOLLY.   Hi.

DAN.   Do you come here often?

MOLLY.   Never.

DAN.   I don't either.

MOLLY.   I'm waiting here for a friend. She selected this place. I think what's happening to the West Side is outrageous.

DAN.   This is really an East Side singles kind of restaurant.

MOLLY.   Yes, but it's here on the West Side, so we have to deal with it.

DAN.   You sound like a concerned citizen.

MOLLY.   Did you ever read any Kenneth Burke? In college, maybe? Lit. Crit.?

DAN.   *(Immediately.)* Oh, sure.

MOLLY.   He divides people into observers, spectators, and participants. I'm here strictly as a sociological observer. I love to watch people in New York. Otherwise I would never come to a place like this.

DAN. I wouldn't either. In my spare time I write film criticism.

MOLLY. *(More interested.)* Oh, you're a critic! Who do you write for?

DAN. I write for myself. I keep a film criticism journal.

MOLLY. I love film. Women in film particularly interest me. My favorites are Diane Kurys, Doris Dörrie, and Lee Grant.

DAN. I love women in film too.

MOLLY. *(Impressed.)* You're so direct and forthcoming. What do you do?

DAN. I'm a psychiatrist.

MOLLY. Individual, group, house calls?

DAN. Actually, I'm a creative director at the B.B.D. & O. advertising agency. But I think of it as psychology. Dealing with the individual's everyday dreams and desires. I'm in charge of the Scott Paper account.

MOLLY. Fascinating. I use tissues a lot. I've always wondered why.

DAN. What do *you* do?

MOLLY. I'm a systems analyst for American Express.

DAN. "Do you know me?"

MOLLY. *(Very straightforward.)* Not very well. But I'd like to.

DAN. *(Looks at her intently.)* Why don't we go somewhere a little less trendy to talk. I can tell these aren't your kind of people.

MOLLY. No, I don't belong here. This isn't my New York.

DAN. *(Helps her on with her coat.)* That's a nice jacket.

MOLLY. Donna Karan. But I've moved on to Issey Miyake.

DAN. *(Putting on a multilayered karate jacket.)* We have so much in common.

MOLLY. "It's a phenomenon." That's a quote from a song in *Gypsy.* "Small world, isn't it?" I love Stephen Sondheim.

DAN. I'm afraid I don't know much about theater. I'm a workaholic. You know, mid-thirties New York guy, longing for Real Relationship with Remarkable Woman, meanwhile finds fulfillment through his work.

MOLLY. I think I like you. But be careful, I have Fear of Intimacy.

DAN. The Bachelor Girl's Disease. I hear it's an epidemic.

MOLLY. I'm working with my shrink to get past it. *(Pause as Dan looks at her.)*

DAN. I think I like you, too. *(They begin to exit restaurant.)* What about your girl friend?

MOLLY. Uh, ah, she told me if she wasn't here by now she wasn't coming.

DAN. Not a very reliable friend.

MOLLY. No, but she's working with her shrink to get past it. *(They exit.)*


## SCENE TWO

*Phil's Risotto, a risotto and cheese emporium. Dan and Molly stroll over to the counter arm in arm. It is mid-September.*


DAN. *(Ordering at the counter.)* We'll have lemon risotto, chanterelle risotto, spinach risotto salad, pesto tart, carrot ravioli, goat cheese, goat cheese with ash, and a half pound of American.

MOLLY. *(Surprised, almost disturbed.)* American?

DAN. Have you ever had real American cheese? Not the stuff they sell at the supermarket, but real American. *(He gives her a piece.)* Taste this.

MOLLY. *(Tasting.)* Oh, that's marvelous!

DAN. I've been rediscovering American food: peanut butter, grape jelly, Marshmallow Fluff, Scooter Pies, Chef Boyardee, bologna. It is unbelievable! If it's done correctly.

MOLLY. *(Softly.)* I love you.

DAN. Excuse me?

MOLLY. I love blue. I adore Kraft blue cheese dressing.

DAN. Well, if it's done correctly.

# SCENE THREE

*Molly in the office of her psychiatrist, Dr. Susan. It is October.*

MOLLY.   *(Sneezes.)* Excuse me. I'm getting a cold.

DR. SUSAN.   How do you feel about that?

MOLLY.   Terrible. Tissues remind me of him. He says people should live together before they get married.

DR. SUSAN.   How do you feel about that?

MOLLY.   Sigourney Weaver and Glenn Close are married.

DR. SUSAN.   How do you feel about that?

MOLLY.   Living together was for kids in the late sixties and seventies. I'm a thirty-three-year-old woman.

DR. SUSAN.   How do you feel about that?

MOLLY.   I need a commitment. I want a family. I don't want to take a course at the New School on how to place a personal ad. Meryl Streep has three children already.

DR. SUSAN.   Why do you always compare yourself to movie stars? You're not an actress.

MOLLY.   That's true. That's really true!! That's an incredible insight. Maybe my mother wanted me to be an actress. I hate her.

# SCENE FOUR

*Dan in the office of his psychologist, Stanley Tannenbaum, Ph.D. It is November.*

DAN.   I don't think I want to make a commitment to Molly, but I'm afraid of what she'll say.

STANLEY TANNENBAUM, PH.D.   Well, let's put Molly in this chair, and then you can answer for her.

DAN. All right. *(Talking now to an empty chair.)* Molly, I don't think I want to make a commitment. *(Dan gets up and sits in chair to answer as Molly would. Pretending he's Molly.)* That's okay. I'm an observer. This is all a sociological investigation. Kenneth Burke divides people into spectators, partici — *(Dan runs back to his seat to answer Molly. Angry.)* Who the hell is Kenneth Burke? That is so pretentious, Molly! *(As Molly.)* Not as pretentious as keeping a journal of film criticisms. *(Furious.)* You resent my writing! You want to swallow me up. If I live with you, I won't be here anymore. I'll lose myself.

STANLEY TANNENBAUM, PH.D. Did you hear what you just said?

DAN. I have it. Goddamn it! I have it. Fear of Intimacy. That Bachelor Girl's Disease. Why couldn't I just get burn-out?

## SCENE FIVE

*Central Park West. The Thanksgiving Day Parade. Dan and Molly are watching floats of Bullwinkle and Superman pass by.*

MOLLY. *(Overcome by the sight of the floats.)* I love this parade. Gosh, I really love this parade. Reminds me of growing up here and of New York before there were Benetton shops and a Trump organization.

DAN. I never imagined people actually grew up in New York.

MOLLY. It was different then. There were real neighborhoods. The ladies on Madison Avenue wore white gloves and ate mashed potatoes at the Kirby Allen Restaurant. Marjorie Morningstar and her family gathered for Sabbath dinners on Central Park West. All artists wore turtlenecks and played bongo drums in the Village. And every night at seven o'clock, men in top hats and tails tap-danced from Shubert Alley to the Winter Garden Theater.

DAN. Really!

MOLLY.   Well, I like to think so. Now everywhere I go all the women look like me.

DAN.   What's so bad about that?

MOLLY.   Nothing, it's just that it's all the same. I like the idea of a flower district, a theater district, a diamond district. The whole city is being renovated into Molly district. Dan, I have to confess. I hate goat cheese.

DAN.   *(Softly.)* Me, too. But I love you.

MOLLY.   Hmmmmmm?

DAN.   I hate goat cheese, but I love blue. Molly, with Bullwinkle as my witness, I want to marry you. And every Thanksgiving we can bring our children here. And someday they'll tell someone they met at The Trading Post, "I love this parade, I grew up here."

MOLLY.   *(No longer wistful.)* But will our children go to Trinity or the Ethical Culture School? They could probably learn Chinese at Trinity, but there are a lot of Wall Street parents. Ethical Culture is nice, but maybe it's too liberal, not enough attention to the classics. How 'bout Brearley? There's something to be said for an all-women's education. *(She kisses Dan.)* Dan, just think! We can raise a family of women filmmakers!!!!!

## SCENE SIX

*The Helmsley palace. The Grand Ballroom. An enormous wedding party. Dan and Molly are standing under the altar before Her Majesty, the Queen.*

QUEEN.   Dan, do you take this woman to be your wife? To love, be emotionally supportive of, have good dialogue with, as well as a country home in the Hamptons, Connecticut, or possibly upper New York State?

DAN.   I do.

QUEEN. Molly, do you take this man to love, and at the same time maintain your career, spend quality time with the children, and keep yourself appealing by joining the New York Health and Racquet Club?

MOLLY. I do.

QUEEN. *(Addressing the wedding guests.)* I've know this couple for two hours. But I've stood guard at their honeymoon suite. Molly will be able to see her makeup in soft light in the bathroom mirror. Dan will be put at ease by the suit hangers that detach from the closet. And if Dan and Molly decide to get remarried someday, and return to the honeymoon suite, I will keep a note of their room number. I wouldn't sleep in a new room, why should they?

DAN. *(Bows.)* Thank you, Your Majesty.

MOLLY. *(Curtsies.)* Thank you, Your Majesty.

QUEEN. And now by virtue of being Queen of all the Helmsleys, I pronounce you husband and wife. Congratulations! You may kiss the bride. *(Dan kisses Molly. There are cheers and the band begins to play a song like "Lullaby of Broadway."\* Five hundred men in top hats and tails begin to tap down the aisle.)*

# EPILOGUE

NARRATOR. Dan and Molly became bi-island (Manhattan and Long), with bi-point three children (a girl, a boy, and an au pair from Barnard), and bi-career (a shift into management for him, a cottage industry for her). As Molly approached middle age she began to consult crystals about her hormonal convergence and undertook frequent pilgrimages to Stonehenge. Dan continued to pursue his interest in early American comestibles, and was featured on the cover of *Just Say Cheese* magazine for his distinguished cellar of American pasteurized-cheese foods.

The fortunes of the Queen, however, followed a crueler path. After a long and glorious reign, she was found to be poaching,

\* See Special Note on Songs and Recordings on copyright page.

thereby violating the charter, and was forced to abdicate. Even a monarch must obey the laws of the realm. On the day she was dethroned, she received a monogrammed Cartier sympathy note from Molly.

> Dear Your Majesty,
> Dan and I send you our best wishes at this difficult time.
>
> > Molly
>
> P.S. Is your estate in Greenwich for sale?

Molly's mother had taught her that a lady always sends a note.

Otherwise — apart from twenty years of couples therapy, his-and-her reconstructive surgery, one triple by-pass, and four extramarital affairs — they lived happily ever after.

# THE MAN IN A CASE

# CHARACTERS

BYELINKOV
VARINKA

# THE MAN IN A CASE

*A small garden in the village of Mironitski. 1898.*

*Byelinkov is pacing. Enter Varinka out of breath.*

BYELINKOV.    You are ten minutes late.

VARINKA.    The most amazing thing happened on my way over here. You know the woman who runs the grocery store down the road. She wears a black wig during the week, and a blond wig on Saturday nights. And she has the daughter who married an engineer in Moscow who is doing very well thank you and is living, God bless them, in a three-room apartment. But he really is the most boring man in the world. All he talks about is his future and his station in life. Well, she heard we were to be married and she gave me this basket of apricots to give to you.

BYELINKOV.    That is a most amazing thing!

VARINKA.    She said to me, Varinka, you are marrying the most honorable man in the entire village. In this village he is the only man fit to speak with my son-in-law.

BYELINKOV.    I don't care for apricots. They give me hives.

VARINKA.    I can return them. I'm sure if I told her they give you hives she would give me a basket of raisins or a cake.

BYELINKOV.    I don't know this woman or her pompous son-in-law. Why would she give me her cakes?

VARINKA.    She adores you!

BYELINKOV.    She is emotionally loose.

VARINKA.    She adores you by reputation. Everyone adores you by reputation. I tell everyone I am to marry Byelinkov, the finest teacher in the county.

BYELINKOV.    You tell them this?

VARINKA.    If they don't tell me first.

BYELINKOV.    Pride can be an imperfect value.

VARINKA.  It isn't pride. It is the truth. You are a great man!

BYELINKOV.  I am the master of Greek and Latin at a local school at the end of the village of Mironitski. *(Varinka kisses him.)*

VARINKA.  And I am to be the master of Greek and Latin's wife!

BYELINKOV.  Being married requires a great deal of responsibility. I hope I am able to provide you with all that a married man must properly provide a wife.

VARINKA.  We will be very happy.

BYELINKOV.  Happiness is for children. We are entering into a social contract, an amicable agreement to provide us with a secure and satisfying future.

VARINKA.  You are so sweet! You are the sweetest man in the world!

BYELINKOV.  I'm a man set in his ways who saw a chance to provide himself with a small challenge.

VARINKA.  Look at you! Look at you! Your sweet round spectacles, your dear collar always starched, always raised, your perfectly pressed pants always creasing at right angles perpendicular to the floor, and my most favorite part, the sweet little galoshes, rain or shine, just in case. My Byelinkov, never taken by surprise. Except by me.

BYELINKOV.  You speak about me as if I were your pet.

VARINKA.  You are my pet! My little school mouse.

BYELINKOV.  A mouse?

VARINKA.  My sweetest dancing bear with galoshes, my little stale babka.

BYELINKOV.  A stale babka?

VARINKA.  I am not Pushkin.

BYELINKOV.  *(Laughs.)* That depends what you think of Pushkin.

VARINKA.  You're smiling. I knew I could make you smile today.

BYELINKOV.  I am a responsible man. Every day I have for breakfast black bread, fruit, hot tea, and every day I smile three times. I am halfway into my translation of the *Aeneid* from classical Greek hexameter into Russian alexandrines. In 20 years I have never been late to school. I am a responsible man, but no dancing bear.

VARINKA.  Dance with me.

BYELINKOV.  Now? It is nearly four weeks before the wedding!
VARINKA.  It's a beautiful afternoon. We are in your garden.
The roses are in full bloom.
BYELINKOV.  The roses have beetles.
VARINKA.  Dance with me!
BYELINKOV.  You are a demanding woman.
VARINKA.  You chose me. And right. And left. And turn. And
right. And left.
BYELINKOV.  And turn. Give me your hand. You dance like a
school mouse. It's a beautiful afternoon! We are in my garden.
The roses are in full bloom! And turn. And turn. *(Twirls Varinka
around.)*
VARINKA.  I am the luckiest woman! *(Byelinkov stops dancing.)*
Why are you stopping?
BYELINKOV.  To place a lilac in your hair. Every year on this day
I will place a lilac in your hair.
VARINKA.  Will you remember?
BYELINKOV.  I will write it down. *(Takes a notebook from his pocket.)*
Dear Byelinkov, don't forget the day a young lady, your bride,
entered your garden, your peace, and danced on the roses. On
that day every year you are to place a lilac in her hair.
VARINKA.  I love you.
BYELINKOV.  It is convenient we met.
VARINKA.  I love you.
BYELINKOV.  You are a girl.
VARINKA.  I am 30.
BYELINKOV.  But you think like a girl. That is an attractive
attribute.
VARINKA.  Do you love me?
BYELINKOV.  We've never spoken about housekeeping.
VARINKA.  I am an excellent housekeeper. I kept house for my
family on the farm in Gadyatchsky. I can make a beetroot soup
with tomatoes and aubergines which is so nice. Awfully awfully
nice.
BYELINKOV.  You are fond of expletives.
VARINKA.  My beet soup, sir, is excellent!
BYELINKOV.  Please don't be cross. I too am an excellent house-
keeper. I have a place for everything in the house. A shelf for each

71

pot, a cubby for every spoon, a folder for favorite recipes. I have cooked for myself for 20 years. Though my beet soup is not outstanding, it is sufficient.

VARINKA.   I'm sure it's very good.

BYELINKOV.   No. It is awfully, awfully not. What I am outstanding in, however, what gives me greatest pleasure, is preserving those things which are left over. I wrap each tomato slice I haven't used in a wet cloth and place it in the coolest corner of the house. I have had my shoes for seven years because I wrap them in the galoshes you are so fond of. And every night before I go to sleep I wrap my bed in quilts and curtains so I never catch a draft.

VARINKA.   You sleep with curtains on your bed?

BYELINKOV.   I like to keep warm.

VARINKA.   I will make you a new quilt.

BYELINKOV.   No. No new quilt. That would be hazardous.

VARINKA.   It is hazardous to sleep under curtains.

BYELINKOV.   Varinka, I don't like change very much. If one works out the arithmetic the final fraction of improvement is at best less than an eighth of value over the total damage caused by disruption. I never thought of marrying till I saw your eyes dancing among the familiar faces at the headmaster's tea. I assumed I would grow old preserved like those which are left over, wrapped suitably in my case of curtains and quilts.

VARINKA.   Byelinkov, I want us to have dinners with friends and summer country visits. I want people to say, "Have you spent time with Varinka and Byelinkov? He is so happy now that they are married. She is just what he needed."

BYELINKOV.   You have already brought me some happiness. But I never was a sad man. Don't ever think I thought I was a sad man.

VARINKA.   My sweetest darling, you can be whatever you want! If you are sad, they'll say she talks all the time, and he is soft-spoken and king.

BYELINKOV.   And if I am difficult?

VARINKA.   Oh, they'll say he is difficult because he is highly intelligent. All great men are difficult. Look at Lermontov, Tchaikovsky, Peter the Great.

BYELINKOV.  Ivan the Terrible.

VARINKA.  Yes, him too.

BYELINKOV.  Why are you marrying me? I am none of these things.

VARINKA.  To me you are.

BYELINKOV.  You have imagined this. You have constructed an elaborate romance for yourself. Perhaps you are the great one. You are the one with the great imagination.

VARINKA.  Byelinkov, I am a pretty girl of 30. You're right, I am not a woman. I have not made myself into a woman because I do not deserve that honor. Until I came to this town to visit my brother I lived on my family's farm. As the years passed I became younger and younger in fear that I would never marry. And it wasn't that I wasn't pretty enough or sweet enough, it was just that no man ever looked at me and saw a wife. I was not the woman who would be there when he came home. Until I met you I thought I would lie all my life and say I never married because I never met a man I loved. I will love you, Byelinkov. And I will help you to love me. We deserve the life everyone else has. We deserve not to be different.

BYELINKOV.  Yes. We are the same as everyone else.

VARINKA.  Tell me you love me.

BYELINKOV.  I love you.

VARINKA.  *(Takes his hands.)* We will be very happy. I am very strong. *(Pauses.)* It is time for tea.

BYELINKOV.  It is too early for tea. Tea is at half past the hour.

VARINKA.  Do you have heavy cream? It will be awfully nice with apricots.

BYELINKOV.  Heavy cream is too rich for teatime.

VARINKA.  But today is special. Today you placed a lilac in my hair. Write in your note pad. Every year we will celebrate with apricots and heavy cream. I will go to my brother's house and get some.

BYELINKOV.  But your brother's house is a mile from here.

VARINKA.  Today it is much shorter. Today my brother gave me his bicycle to ride. I will be back very soon.

BYELINKOV.  You rode to my house by bicycle! Did anyone see you?

73

VARINKA.   Of course. I had such fun. I told you I saw the grocery store lady with the son-in-law who is doing very well thank you in Moscow, and the headmaster's wife.

BYELINKOV.   You saw the headmaster's wife!

VARINKA.   She smiled at me.

BYELINKOV.   Did she laugh or smile?

VARINKA.   She laughed a little. She said, "My dear, you are very progressive to ride a bicycle." She said you and your fiancé Byelinkov must ride together sometime. I wonder if he'll take off his galoshes when he rides a bicycle.

BYELINKOV.   She said that?

VARINKA.   She adores you. We had a good giggle.

BYELINKOV.   A woman can be arrested for riding a bicycle. That is not progressive, it is a premeditated revolutionary act. Your brother must be awfully, awfully careful on behalf of your behavior. He has been careless — oh so careless — in giving you the bicycle.

VARINKA.   Dearest Byelinkov, you are wrapping yourself under curtains and quilts! I made friends on the bicycle.

BYELINKOV.   You saw more than the headmaster's wife and the idiot grocery woman.

VARINKA.   She is not an idiot.

BYELINKOV.   She is a potato-vending, sausage-armed fool!

VARINKA.   Shhh! My school mouse. Shhh!

BYELINKOV.   What other friends did you make on this bicycle?

VARINKA.   I saw students from my brother's classes. They waved and shouted, "Anthropos in love! Anthropos in love!!"

BYELINKOV.   Where is that bicycle?

VARINKA.   I left it outside the gate. Where are you going?

BYELINKOV.   *(Muttering as he exits.)* Anthropos in love, anthropos in love.

VARINKA.   They were cheering me on. Careful, you'll trample the roses.

BYELINKOV.   *(Returning with the bicycle.)* Anthropos is the Greek singular for man. Anthropos in love translates as the Greek and Latin master in love. Of course they cheered you. Their instructor who teaches them the discipline and contained beauty of the

74

classics, is in love with a sprite on a bicycle. It is a good giggle, isn't it? A very good giggle! I am returning this bicycle to your brother.

VARINKA.     But it is teatime.

BYELINKOV.     Today we will not have tea.

VARINKA.     But you will have to walk back a mile.

BYELINKOV.     I have my galoshes on. *(Gets on the bicycle.)* Varinka, we deserve not to be different. *(Begins to pedal. The bicycle doesn't move.)*

VARINKA.     Put the kickstand up.

BYELINKOV.     I beg your pardon.

VARINKA.     *(Giggling.)* Byelinkov, to make the bicycle move, you must put the kickstand up. *(Byelinkov puts it up and awkwardly falls off the bicycle as it moves. Varinka laughing.)* Ha ha ha. My little school mouse. You look so funny! You are the sweetest dearest man in the world. Ha ha ha! *(Pause.)*

BYELINKOV.     Please help me up. I'm afraid my galosh is caught.

VARINKA.     *(Trying not to laugh.)* Your galosh is caught! *(Explodes in laughter again.)* Oh, you are so funny! I do love you so. *(Helps Byelinkov up.)* You were right, my pet, as always. We don't need heavy cream for tea. The fraction of improvement isn't worth the damage caused by the disruption.

BYELINKOV.     Varinka, it is still too early for tea. I must complete two stanzas of my translation before late afternoon. That is my regular schedule.

VARINKA.     Then I will watch while you work.

BYELINKOV.     No. You had a good giggle. That is enough.

VARINKA.     Then while you work I will work too. I will make lists of guests for our wedding.

BYELINKOV.     I can concentrate only when I am alone in my house. Please take your bicycle home to your brother.

VARINKA.     But I don't want to leave you. You look so sad.

BYELINKOV.     I never was a sad man. Don't ever think I was a sad man.

VARINKA.     Byelinkov, it's a beautiful day, we are in your garden. The roses are in bloom.

BYELINKOV.     Allow me to help you on to your bicycle. *(Takes Varinka's hand as she gets on the bike.)*

VARINKA.    You are such a gentleman. We will be very happy.

BYELINKOV.    You are very strong. Good day, Varinka. *(Varinka pedals off. Byelinkov, alone in the garden, takes out his pad and rips up the note about the lilac, strews it over the garden, then carefully picks up each piece of paper and places them all in a small envelope as lights fade to black.)*

# NEW PLAYS

★ **MONTHS ON END by Craig Pospisil.** In comic scenes, one for each month of the year, we follow the intertwined worlds of a circle of friends and family whose lives are poised between happiness and heartbreak. "...a triumph...these twelve vignettes all form crucial pieces in the eternal puzzle known as human relationships, an area in which the playwright displays an assured knowledge that spans deep sorrow to unbounded happiness." —*Ann Arbor News.* "...rings with emotional truth, humor...[an] endearing contemplation on love...entertaining and satisfying." —*Oakland Press.* [5M, 5W] ISBN: 0-8222-1892-5

★ **GOOD THING by Jessica Goldberg.** Brings us into the households of John and Nancy Roy, forty-something high-school guidance counselors whose marriage has been increasingly on the rocks and Dean and Mary, recent graduates struggling to make their way in life. "...a blend of gritty social drama, poetic humor and unsubtle existential contemplation..." —*Variety.* [3M, 3W] ISBN: 0-8222-1869-0

★ **THE DEAD EYE BOY by Angus MacLachlan.** Having fallen in love at their Narcotics Anonymous meeting, Billy and Shirley-Diane are striving to overcome the past together. But their relationship is complicated by the presence of Sorin, Shirley-Diane's fourteen-year-old son, a damaged reminder of her dark past. "...a grim, insightful portrait of an unmoored family..." —*NY Times.* "MacLachlan's play isn't for the squeamish, but then, tragic stories delivered at such an unrelenting fever pitch rarely are." —*Variety.* [1M, 1W, 1 boy] ISBN: 0-8222-1844-5

★ **[SIC] by Melissa James Gibson.** In adjacent apartments three young, ambitious neighbors come together to discuss, flirt, argue, share their dreams and plan their futures with unequal degrees of deep hopefulness and abject despair. "A work...concerned with the sound and power of language..." —*NY Times.* "...a wonderfully original take on urban friendship and the comedy of manners—a *Design for Living* for our times..." —*NY Observer.* [3M, 2W] ISBN: 0-8222-1872-0

★ **LOOKING FOR NORMAL by Jane Anderson.** Roy and Irma's twenty-five-year marriage is thrown into turmoil when Roy confesses that he is actually a woman trapped in a man's body, forcing the couple to wrestle with the meaning of their marriage and the delicate dynamics of family. "Jane Anderson's bittersweet transgender domestic comedy-drama ...is thoughtful and touching and full of wit and wisdom. A real audience pleaser." —*Hollywood Reporter.* [5M, 4W] ISBN: 0-8222-1857-7

★ **ENDPAPERS by Thomas McCormack.** The regal Joshua Maynard, the old and ailing head of a mid-sized, family-owned book-publishing house in New York City, must name a successor. One faction in the house backs a smart, "pragmatic" manager, the other faction a smart, "sensitive" editor and both factions fear what the other's man could do to this house— and to them. "If Kaufman and Hart had undertaken a comedy about the publishing business, they might have written *Endpapers*...a breathlessly fast, funny, and thoughtful comedy ...keeps you amused, guessing, and often surprised...profound in its empathy for the paradoxes of human nature." —*NY Magazine.* [7M, 4W] ISBN: 0-8222-1908-5

★ **THE PAVILION by Craig Wright.** By turns poetic and comic, romantic and philosophical, this play asks old lovers to face the consequences of difficult choices made long ago. "The script's greatest strength lies in the genuineness of its feeling." —*Houston Chronicle.* "Wright's perceptive, gently witty writing makes this familiar situation fresh and thoroughly involving." —*Philadelphia Inquirer.* [2M, 1W (flexible casting)] ISBN: 0-8222-1898-4

**DRAMATISTS PLAY SERVICE, INC.**
**440 Park Avenue South, New York, NY 10016  212-683-8960  Fax 212-213-1539**
**postmaster@dramatists.com   www.dramatists.com**

# NEW PLAYS

★ **BE AGGRESSIVE by Annie Weisman.** Vista Del Sol is paradise, sandy beaches, avocado-lined streets. But for seventeen-year-old cheerleader Laura, everything changes when her mother is killed in a car crash, and she embarks on a journey to the Spirit Institute of the South where she can learn "cheer" with Bible belt intensity. "...filled with lingual gymnastics...stylized rapid-fire dialogue..." –*Variety*. "...a new, exciting, and unique voice in the American theatre..." –*BackStage West*. [1M, 4W, extras] ISBN: 0-8222-1894-1

★ **FOUR by Christopher Shinn.** Four people struggle desperately to connect in this quiet, sophisticated, moving drama. "...smart, broken-hearted...Mr. Shinn has a precocious and forgiving sense of how power shifts in the game of sexual pursuit...He promises to be a playwright to reckon with..." –*NY Times*. "A voice emerges from an American place. It's got humor, sadness and a fresh and touching rhythm that tell of the loneliness and secrets of life...[a] poetic, haunting play." –*NY Post*. [3M, 1W] ISBN: 0-8222-1850-X

★ **WONDER OF THE WORLD by David Lindsay-Abaire.** A madcap picaresque involving Niagara Falls, a lonely tour-boat captain, a pair of bickering private detectives and a husband's dirty little secret. "Exceedingly whimsical and playfully wicked. Winning and genial. A top-drawer production." –*NY Times*. "Full frontal lunacy is on display. A most assuredly fresh and hilarious tragicomedy of marital discord run amok...absolutely hysterical..." –*Variety*. [3M, 4W (doubling)] ISBN: 0-8222-1863-1

★ **QED by Peter Parnell.** Nobel Prize-winning physicist and all-around genius Richard Feynman holds forth with captivating wit and wisdom in this fascinating biographical play that originally starred Alan Alda. "QED is a seductive mix of science, human affections, moral courage, and comic eccentricity. It reflects on, among other things, death, the absence of God, travel to an unexplored country, the pleasures of drumming, and the need to know and understand." –*NY Magazine*. "Its rhythms correspond to the way that people—even geniuses—approach and avoid highly emotional issues, and it portrays Feynman with affection and awe." –*The New Yorker*. [1M, 1W] ISBN: 0-8222-1924-7

★ **UNWRAP YOUR CANDY by Doug Wright.** Alternately chilling and hilarious, this deliciously macabre collection of four bedtime tales for adults is guaranteed to keep you awake for nights on end. "Engaging and intellectually satisfying...a treat to watch." –*NY Times*. "Fiendishly clever. Mordantly funny and chilling. Doug Wright teases, freezes and zaps us." –*Village Voice*. "Four bite-size plays that bite back." –*Variety*. [flexible casting] ISBN: 0-8222-1871-2

★ **FURTHER THAN THE FURTHEST THING by Zinnie Harris.** On a remote island in the middle of the Atlantic secrets are buried. When the outside world comes calling, the islanders find their world blown apart from the inside as well as beyond. "Harris winningly produces an intimate and poetic, as well as political, family saga." –*Independent (London)*. "Harris' enthralling adventure of a play marks a departure from stale, well-furrowed theatrical terrain." –*Evening Standard (London)*. [3M, 2W] ISBN: 0-8222-1874-7

★ **THE DESIGNATED MOURNER by Wallace Shawn.** The story of three people living in a country where what sort of books people like to read and how they choose to amuse themselves becomes both firmly personal and unexpectedly entangled with questions of survival. "This is a playwright who does not just tell you what it is like to be arrested at night by goons or to fall morally apart and become an aimless yet weirdly contented ghost yourself. He has the originality to make you feel it." –*Times (London)*. "A fascinating play with beautiful passages of writing..." –*Variety*. [2M, 1W] ISBN: 0-8222-1848-8

**DRAMATISTS PLAY SERVICE, INC.**
440 Park Avenue South, New York, NY 10016  212-683-8960  Fax 212-213-1539
postmaster@dramatists.com  www.dramatists.com

# NEW PLAYS

★ **SHEL'S SHORTS by Shel Silverstein.** Lauded poet, songwriter and author of children's books, the incomparable Shel Silverstein's short plays are deeply infused with the same wicked sense of humor that made him famous. "...[a] childlike honesty and twisted sense of humor." *–Boston Herald.* "...terse dialogue and an absurdity laced with a tang of dread give [*Shel's Shorts*] more than a trace of Samuel Beckett's comic existentialism." *–Boston Phoenix.* [flexible casting] ISBN: 0-8222-1897-6

★ **AN ADULT EVENING OF SHEL SILVERSTEIN by Shel Silverstein.** Welcome to the darkly comic world of Shel Silverstein, a world where nothing is as it seems and where the most innocent conversation can turn menacing in an instant. These ten imaginative plays vary widely in content, but the style is unmistakable. "...[*An Adult Evening*] shows off Silverstein's virtuosic gift for wordplay...[and] sends the audience out...with a clear appreciation of human nature as perverse and laughable." *–NY Times.* [flexible casting] ISBN: 0-8222-1873-9

★ **WHERE'S MY MONEY? by John Patrick Shanley.** A caustic and sardonic vivisection of the institution of marriage, laced with the author's inimitable razor-sharp wit. "...Shanley's gift for acid-laced one-liners and emotionally tumescent exchanges is certainly potent..." *–Variety.* "...lively, smart, occasionally scary and rich in reverse wisdom." *–NY Times.* [3M, 3W] ISBN: 0-8222-1865-8

★ **A FEW STOUT INDIVIDUALS by John Guare.** A wonderfully screwy comedy-drama that figures Ulysses S. Grant in the throes of writing his memoirs, surrounded by a cast of fantastical characters, including the Emperor and Empress of Japan, the opera star Adelina Patti and Mark Twain. "Guare's smarts, passion and creativity skyrocket to awesome heights..." *–Star Ledger.* "...precisely the kind of good new play that you might call an everyday miracle...every minute of it is fresh and newly alive..." *–Village Voice.* [10M, 3W] ISBN: 0-8222-1907-7

★ **BREATH, BOOM by Kia Corthron.** A look at fourteen years in the life of Prix, a Bronx native, from her ruthless girl-gang leadership at sixteen through her coming to maturity at thirty. "...vivid world, believable and eye-opening, a place worthy of a dramatic visit, where no one would want to live but many have to." *–NY Times.* "...rich with humor, terse vernacular strength and gritty detail..." *–Variety.* [1M, 9W] ISBN: 0-8222-1849-6

★ **THE LATE HENRY MOSS by Sam Shepard.** Two antagonistic brothers, Ray and Earl, are brought together after their father, Henry Moss, is found dead in his seedy New Mexico home in this classic Shepard tale. "...His singular gift has been for building mysteries out of the ordinary ingredients of American family life..." *–NY Times.* "...rich moments ...Shepard finds gold." *–LA Times.* [7M, 1W] ISBN: 0-8222-1858-5

★ **THE CARPETBAGGER'S CHILDREN by Horton Foote.** One family's history spanning from the Civil War to WWII is recounted by three sisters in evocative, intertwining monologues. "...bittersweet music—[a] rhapsody of ambivalence...in its modest, garrulous way...theatrically daring." *–The New Yorker.* [3W] ISBN: 0-8222-1843-7

★ **THE NINA VARIATIONS by Steven Dietz.** In this funny, fierce and heartbreaking homage to *The Seagull*, Dietz puts Chekhov's star-crossed lovers in a room and doesn't let them out. "A perfect little jewel of a play..." *–Shepherdstown Chronicle.* "...a delightful revelation of a writer at play; and also an odd, haunting, moving theater piece of lingering beauty." *–Eastside Journal (Seattle).* [1M, 1W (flexible casting)] ISBN: 0-8222-1891-7

**DRAMATISTS PLAY SERVICE, INC.**
**440 Park Avenue South, New York, NY 10016  212-683-8960  Fax 212-213-1539**
**postmaster@dramatists.com  www.dramatists.com**